Great Moments of Our Time

GREAT MOMENTS OF OUR TIME

★ *Volume I* ★

Events That Changed
Our World...
And Sometimes Touched
Our Hearts

Edited by
Robert Aldace Wood
Illustrated by
Steven Carter

Hallmark Editions

Landmarks
Of Personal Achievement

APPOINTMENT WITH DESTINY

The Baltimore Sun *said of him, "He has exalted the race of men." Indeed, Charles Lindbergh's three-thousand-mile solo crossing of the Atlantic was a feat unmatched for skill and courage. His achievement electrified the world and won him international praise. But all of this lay in the undreamt future. Now, here in his own words, Lindbergh tells what went through his mind in the final critical moments of his solo epic.*

I've never landed the *Spirit of St. Louis* at night before. It would be better to come in straight. But if I don't sideslip, I'll be too high over the boundary to touch my wheels in the area of light. That would mean circling again—Still too high. I push the stick over to a steeper slip, leaving the nose well down—Below the hangar roofs now—straighten out—A short burst of the engine—Over the lighted area—Sod coming up to meet me—Deceptive high lights and shadows—Careful—easy to bounce when you're tired—Still too fast—Tail too high—Hold off—Hold off...The wheels touch gently—off again—No, I'll keep contact—Ease the stick forward—Back on the ground—Off—Back—the tail skid too—Not a bad landing, but I'm beyond the light—can't see anything ahead—Like flying in fog—Ground loop?—No, still rolling too fast—might blow a tire—The field *must* be clear—Uncomfortable though, jolting into blackness…Slower, now—slow enough to ground loop safely—left rudder—reverse it—stick over the other way—The *Spirit of St. Louis* swings around and stops rolling, resting on the solidness of earth, in the center of Le Bourget.

I start to taxi back toward the floodlights and hangars—But the entire field ahead is covered with running figures!

…When I circled the aerodrome it did not occur to me that any connection existed between my arrival and the cars stalled in traffic on the roads. When my wheels touched earth, I had no way of knowing that tens of thousands of men and women were breaking down fences and flooding past guards.

I had barely cut the engine switch when the first people reached my cockpit. Within seconds my open windows were blocked with faces. My name was called out over and over again, in accents strange to my ears—on this side of my plane—on that side—in front—in the distance. I could feel the *Spirit of St. Louis* tremble with the pressure of the crowd….

"Are there any mechanics here?" I asked.

I couldn't understand a single word that came back in answer—from a half-dozen different mouths.

"Does anyone here speak English?" I shouted....

I opened the door, and started to put my foot down onto ground. But dozens of hands took hold of me—my legs, my arms, my body. No one heard the sentences I spoke. I found myself lying in a prostrate position, up on top of the crowd, in the center of an ocean of heads that extended as far out into the darkness as I could see. Then I started to sink down into that ocean, and was buoyed up again. Thousands of voices mingled in a roar. Men were shouting, stumbling. My head and shoulders went down, and up, and down again, and up once more. It was like drowning in a human sea. I lost sight of the *Spirit of St. Louis.* I heard several screams. I was afraid that I would be dropped under the feet of those milling, cheering people; and that after sitting in a cockpit-fixed position for close to thirty-four hours, my muscles would be too stiff to struggle up again....

After the lapse of minutes whose number I cannot judge, I felt my helmet jerked from my head. Firmer hands gripped on my body. I heard my name more clearly spoken. And suddenly I was standing on my feet—on European ground at last. With arms linked solidly in mine, I began moving slowly, but unnoticed, through the crowd....

I woke that afternoon, a little stiff but well rested, into a life which could hardly have been more amazing if I had landed on another planet instead of at Paris. The welcome I received at Le Bourget was only a forerunner to the welcome extended by France, by Belgium, by England — and, through messages, by all of Europe. It was a welcome which words of appreciation are incompetent to cover.

★ ★ ★

A GIANT LEAP FOR MANKIND

July 20, 1969 — An earthman, Neil Armstrong, walked on the satellite Moon, saying, "That's one small step for a man, one giant leap for mankind." That historic moment was shared in the homes of millions throughout the world. But nowhere was the drama as thick, as vibrant and poignant, as in the homes of the astronauts' families.

Her fingers gripped so tightly they were almost purple; his hands constantly clenched and opened. When the LM touched the moon, she said, "They're on; they're on!" and he reached over and kissed her. A long wait and then she said, "There go his feet," and she closed her eyes and cried before her son Neil stepped down. Watching him later, she was sure she could see his footprints. She was certain he was crying when he spoke with the President. And when it all crowded in upon her, Viola Armstrong said quietly: "He's so far away."

As the voice from Houston Control crackled over the speakers of 40 million television sets — "Eagle, you are go for powered descent" — the tension, which had built for five days, rose to an excruciating pitch. Nowhere more than in the fieldstone ranch house in Wapakoneta, Ohio. Stephen and Viola Armstrong sat watching it all. They were surrounded by neighbors and relatives who brought home-cooked snacks the way small-town folks do. Yet, in another way, they were alone in the hushed room.

As the Armstrongs watched, memories intersticed the apprehension — how Neil as a young boy would go with other children and look at the moon through a neighbor's telescope. A glance had been enough for the others, but Neil would "look and look and look." How, as a teen-ager, he insisted on flying even after a friend crashed in a field and died in his arms. He'd always been a flier.

In other rooms, three women and their children were watching too, just as solitary and strained almost beyond endurance: Joan Aldrin, Jan Armstrong and Pat Collins. But when the LM rocketed to a landing, anxiety turned to exaltation. "Come on, trolley!" yelled Jan Armstrong. And as the two men walked on the moon, Pat Collins exclaimed, "Why aren't they cheering? That's why they don't send a woman to the moon — she'd jump up and down and yell and weep!"

* * *

THEY SAID
IT COULDN'T BE DONE

In 1908, history's longest international automobile race was run from Times Square to Paris. The contesting vehicles, primitive behemoths from the United States, Germany, France and Italy, ground and plowed their way across America, Japan, Siberia, Russia and the European continent. A Thomas Flyer, driven by George Schuster, carried "the hope of the American automobile industry" to victory and simultaneously to the threshold of the automobile age. Here Schuster recalls what it was like at the finish line.

Rolling at 50 miles an hour over a cobblestone road, we approached Paris. Nobody knew our schedule, but beginning at Meaux, 25 miles out, crowds began to cheer us. Bicyclists rode excitedly alongside. At the city gates, we paid a tax on the gasoline in our tanks. People tossed flowers to us. Summer evening diners in sidewalk cafés raised their glasses and shouted "Vive la voiture américaine."

Gendarmes stopped us and told us that we needed a lamp. A Frenchman gallantly offered one from his bicycle. When it could not be detached, the bicycle was lifted into the car and we continued on our way to more cheers.

Crowds jammed the Boulevard Poissonnière as we stopped the travel-worn Thomas in front of the office of *Le Matin* at 6 P.M., 169 days after leaving New York....It was several weeks before the race committee officially decided in our favor, but we claimed victory at once, and the French gave us a great reception at the Grand Hôtel on the Boulevard des Capucines. There was champagne and more champagne....

Great turnpikes and wide throughways now run where our Thomas Flyer struggled in the snow through New York, Pennsylvania, Ohio, and Indiana. Where we bogged in midwest mud, traffic now speeds all year over Highway 30. It is possible now to drive from Valdez to Fairbanks, Alaska, Owen Meals writes me, in any season, over paved highways, in only seven or eight hours; and you can drive from there to anywhere in the United States or Canada, winter or summer. I like to think that the race back in 1908 was at least a little responsible for all this.

★ ★ ★

THE WOMAN VOTER ARRIVES

On August 18, 1920, Tennessee became the thirty-sixth state to ratify the Nineteenth Amendment to the Constitution of the United States. Woman suffrage was now the law of the land. Today, more than fifty years later, we tend to forget what a burning and divisive issue was woman suffrage. Ten days after ratification, the Literary Digest *printed this roundup of opinion which spotlights the hope and bitterness both that heralded the advent of the woman voter.*

"Tennessee has triumphantly closed the sixty years of women's struggle for the right to have their prayers counted on Election day," says Mrs. Carrie Chapman Catt, president of the National Woman Suffrage Association. "Hell is going to break loose in Georgia if the Suffrage Amendment is ratified," predicted Speaker Walker, leader of the opposition in the Tennessee legislature; "this is now a white man's country and we have a white man's God." "American democracy, won for the white men by the Revolution, extended to all men by the Civil War, is completed by the woman's victory to-day throughout the United States," says Alice Paul, president of the National Woman's party. "Suffrage atavists have brought

us toward the stage of squaw-right reached five thousand years ago by the Hittites just before annihilation and by every other decaying civilization," declares *The Woman Patriot* (Washington, D.C.), an organ of the National Association Opposed to Woman Suffrage. Thus speak leading friends and foes of votes for women....But for the importance of its provisions, as the Newark *Ledger* observes, "the Nineteenth Amendment easily holds first place among formal changes made to this country's fundamental statutes." "The victory is not a victory for women alone," says the Kansas City *Star*, "it is a victory for democracy and the principle of equality upon which the nation was founded. As such it has an even greater meaning than the surface one most apparent. It means that our democracy is still in the process of growth, still capable of renewing its life and vigor and of adapting itself to the new requirements of a progressing age."

National political party leaders, the Presidential candidates, and President Wilson responded to appeals for influence to secure ratification by the Tennessee legislature. After ratification Mr. Cox said:

"The civilization of the world is saved. The mothers of America will stay the hand of war and repudiate those who trifle with a great principle...."

...Mrs. Catt says:

"In this hour of victory there is but one regret

and that is that every man and woman in the nation does not share our joy. To-day there are those yet too blinded by prejudice to recognize the justice and inevitability of woman suffrage, but to-morrow we know that we shall work together for the common good of this great and glorious nation."...

The Louisville *Courier-Journal* calls the Tennessee suffrage action "a triumph which was inevitable, because the fight for it was a fight of reason, of justice, of civilization":

"Persons now alive will live long enough to look back upon the time when women were denied the ballot with something of the sense of detached wonder with which now we look back upon the time when human beings were denied their liberty, or the times when the world fancied itself at the zenith of progressive achievement without the telephone, the telegraph, or the steam-engine."

★ ★ ★

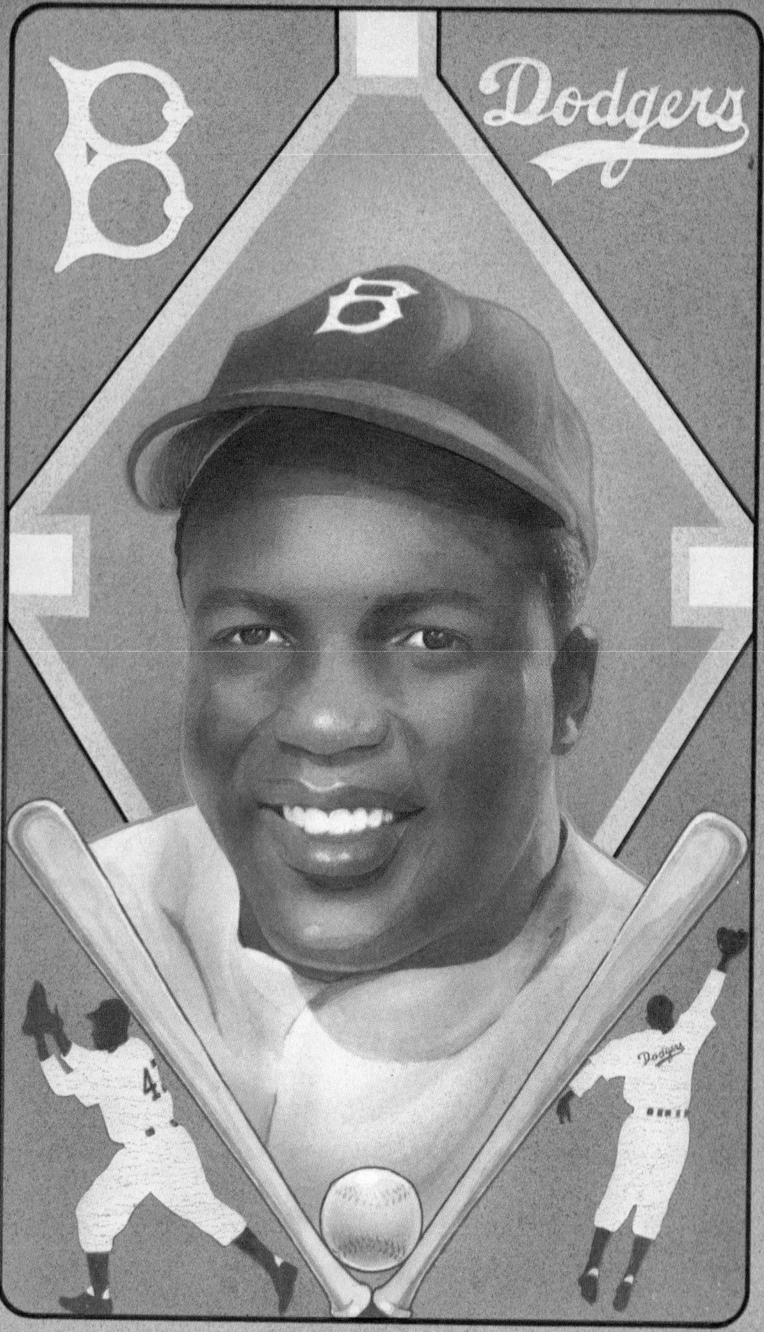
Dodgers
Dodgers

TOUGH ENOUGH TO TAKE IT

Breaking the color barrier in baseball was a coura-geous achievement for the man, Jackie Robinson, and the man who made it possible — Branch Rickey. Here, Arthur Mann recalls the tempestu-ous interview between Robinson and Rickey, pres-ident of the Brooklyn Dodgers.

"Do you know why you were brought here?"

"Not exactly. I heard something about a colored team at Ebbets Field. That it?"

"No...that isn't it." Rickey studied the dark face, the half-open mouth, the widened and wor-ried eyes. Then he said, "You were brought here, Jackie, to play for the Brooklyn organization. Per-haps on Montreal to start with —"

"Me? Play for Montreal?" the player gasped.

Rickey nodded. "If you can make it, yes. Later on — also if you can make it — you'll have a chance with the Brooklyn Dodgers."

Robinson could only nod at this point.

"I want to win pennants and we need ballplay-ers!" Rickey whacked the desk. He sketched the efforts and the scope of his two-year search for players of promise. "Do *you* think you can do it? Make good in organized baseball?"

Robinson shifted to relieve his mounting tension.

"If...if I got the chance," he stammered.

"There's more here than just *playing*, Jackie," Rickey warned. "I wish it meant only hits, runs and errors — things you can see in a box score...."

"Can you do it? Can you do it?" Rickey asked over and over.

Shifting nervously, Robinson looked from Rickey to Sukeforth as they talked of his arms and legs and swing and courage. Did he have the guts to play the game no matter what happened? Rickey pointed out the enormity of the responsibility for all concerned: owners of the club, Rickey, Robinson and all baseball. The opposition would shout insults, come in spikes first, throw at his head.

"Mr. Rickey," Robinson said, "they've been throwing at my head for a long time."

Rickey's voice rose. "Suppose I'm a player...in the heat of an important ball game." He drew back as if to charge at Robinson. "Suppose I collide with you at second base. When I get up, I yell, 'You dirty, black son of a —'" He finished the castigation and added calmly, "What do you do?"

Robinson blinked. He licked his lips and swallowed.

"Mr. Rickey," he murmured, "do you want a ballplayer who's afraid to fight back?"

"I want a ballplayer with guts enough *not* to fight back!" Rickey exclaimed almost savagely.

He paced across the floor and returned with finger pointing. "You've got to do this job with base hits and stolen bases and fielding ground balls, Jackie. *Nothing else!*"...

"Now I'm playing against you in a World Series!" Rickey stormed and removed his jacket for greater freedom. Robinson's hands clenched, trembled from the rising tension. "I'm a hotheaded player. I want to win that game, so I go into you spikes first, but you don't give ground. You stand there and you jab the ball into my ribs and the umpire yells, 'Out!' I flare up — all I see is your face — that black face right on top of me —"

Rickey's bespectacled face, glistening with sweat, was inches from Robinson's at this point. He yelled into the motionless mask, "So I haul off and punch you right in the cheek!"

An oversized fist swung through the air and barely missed Robinson's face. He blinked, but his head didn't move.

"What do you do?" Rickey roared.

"Mr. Rickey," he whispered, "I've got two cheeks. That it?"

On April 10, 1947, Branch Rickey announced: The Brooklyn Dodgers today purchased the contract of Jackie Roosevelt Robinson from the Montreal Royals. He will report immediately.

★ ★ ★

GREAT SCOTT!
IT LOOKS LIKE...
AN EXECUTION!

When the Wright brothers first flew at Kitty Hawk, the New York Tribune *relegated this scientific breakthrough to a short squib on the sports page — underneath an account of a sandlot football game in Brooklyn. Skeptics remained unconvinced. But the day would come when the world would applaud the efforts of these pioneer aviators. That day came on July 30, 1909, in Fort Myer, Virginia, when a Wright brothers' flight fulfilled government tests and proved the practical value of the airplane. It was a moment made for history. Thousands watched breathlessly. Reporter William Inglis gives this eyewitness account.*

The sun was shining brilliantly after a midday of heavy rain. In the new washed blue sky a few cottony clouds were floating indolently. Seven thousand weary Americans were waiting on the dry, brown grass of the tableland at Fort Myer, slowly fanning themselves with their hats until the fierce rays of the sun made their heads throb, then patiently putting their hats back on their heads and dabbing their necks and faces with handkerchiefs already moist. One question was in every mind — would Orville Wright fly quickly and safely to Alexandria and back, carrying an officer of the Signal Corps in his aeroplane, thereby qualifying his machine as a part of the apparatus of the United States Army?...

From afar the aeroplane shed looks like any dingy old barn of unpainted, weather-beaten wood; but as we drew near we became aware of the cause of the spell that was drawing the glance of every eye for miles around. The main door, or, rather, the entire north end of the shed, was wide open, and we could see the flying machine in repose. At the first glance it seemed like a very big dragon-fly that had settled down for rest in a quiet corner of a cigar box. It was so slim, so frail, so attenuated, that one could not imagine it much stronger than a dragon-fly in spite of its great spread of wings; and the mere thought of two men trusting themselves to the support of this delicate, cobwebby thing in a flight through space at the rate of nearly a mile a minute was enough to make the hardiest adventurer shudder....

...Nevertheless one could not help feeling that the development and perfection of the aeroplane was inevitable; that, no matter who might be hurt during its progress, the machine must prove a success....

As our car sped back to its position beside the President's tent every member of the party was full of wonder at what we had seen and heard.

"I never expected to have such a treat as this," said the philosopher; "never thought I'd be able to step into the cage and have the great aeroplane bird come up and eat out of my hand. Wish they'd take me up for a flight."

"I'd rather dive off a Block Island sloop into a school of sharks," was the instant reply of another. And these comments are cited only because they illustrate the spirit of the great throng gathered to witness the flight. While three-quarters of the assemblage were shuddering in anticipation of some awful mishap the other quarter were hoping against hope that they, too, could persuade brother Orville or brother Wilbur to take them up in the air....

"Get in," said Orville, and Lieutenant Foulois climbed up among the mazes of steel wires and sat down on a little bit of a flat perch about half as big as the lid of a cracker-box. Think of flying for miles on such a ridiculous saddle! Orville took the other perch at his side and grasped the levers. A brown line of soldiers walked off slowly and solemnly with the rope that hauled up to the top of a derrick a great iron weight. When tripped it would plunge down, and its impetus would haul a line to catapult the aeroplane swiftly forward.

"Great Scott! It looks like the preliminaries of an execution," exclaimed a nervous man who had wrapped his arms around his ribs as if to keep his heart from pounding through.

"O.K.!" brother Orville replied from his perch.

At the same instant the crash of the falling weight and the sharp barking of the engine blended in one roar, as the great war eagle with wings widespread and propellers revolving was launched southward along the monorail. Every heart stood still as the monster swooped down hill parallel to the ground; but this was only for an instant of time, for almost immediately it responded to the upward tilt of the little pair of horizontal planes in front and rose steadily in the air. Sharply the aeroplane turned to the left, and, constantly rising, came flying northward up the field toward us. And that was a moment to be treasured — the first sight of a flying machine made by man rushing forward in mid-air at terrific speed, yet as obedient to the controlling mind as a gentle horse to the touch of the master's hand.

★　★　★

QUEEN
OF THE WATERS

To go where no one has gone before; to dare to do what skeptics decry as impossible — this is a special sort of challenge. And when someone has the audacity to accept the challenge and prove the skeptics wrong, the world takes notice. Only a handful of adventurers have swum the English Channel. Their names are lost to history. But nearly everyone remembers Gertrude Ederle and the day in 1926 when she became the first woman ever to conquer the Channel.

Football and baseball players, champion pugilists and runners, have the roar of the crowd to stimulate flagging energy or as an incentive to victory. There is a tonic in the enthusiasm of thousands of spectators which quickens the spirit and gives tired muscles fresh endurance. Most players do their best before packed stands.

Gertrude Ederle had no such aid to glory. The voices of the few persons on the accompanying tugs were faint in that wilderness of water. Her main encouragement was the thin notes of a phonograph, playing a popular tune.

Yet this nineteen-year-old girl faced an adversary mighty enough to twist and tear the steel of ships, an enemy capable of blows beside which

the pounding of a trip-hammer is less than the falling of a butterfly's wing. She battled a foe stronger than an army with banners, but, like that one who crossed the Rubicon, she came and saw and conquered. She not only conquered the Channel, but she did it on her second attempt and broke the time record for the swim by almost two hours.

At nine minutes after seven o'clock on an August morning, before women of leisure had risen from soft beds to take warm and scented baths and make a leisurely breakfast, this young American girl, smeared with half an inch of unpleasant grease to keep the warmth of life in her body and wearing goggles to keep the briny water from irritating her eyes to the point of blindness, waded into the icy waters which sweep against the rocks of Griz Nez and grimly struck out for the distant shore of England. Twenty miles of water lay between her and her goal — twenty miles of water that sweeping tides and whirling currents were apt to make half as long again! One small girl was going forth to battle the protecting belt which has ever been among the main defenses of the British Isles; one small girl, an atom on the heaving bosom of the sea.

There is no better place than mid-channel for a swimmer to contemplate the insignificance of humankind. It is bleak beyond words and lonely beyond imagining. Melancholy broods out there.... Nothing seems to matter. The impulse is to cease all effort and drift, as a derelict drifts, with the wind and tides. It takes a stout body to keep on, and a stouter heart....

It always was maintained that no woman ever would swim the Channel. No woman was supposed to have the strength or the stubborn courage necessary for this feat, which just about touches the limit of human endeavor. It remained for Gertrude Ederle to prove the fallacy of this idea and to demonstrate that in this branch of sport women are the equals of men....

...When she entered the water at Griz Nez the weather conditions were all that could be asked. ...By noon a wind had stirred the water to choppy waves, and a few hours later such a heavy rain fell that the decks of the tugs were almost untenable. So bad was the weather and so tempestuous the sea that at one time her trainer, old Bill Burgess, wished to take her from the water, but her sister Margaret insisted that she be permitted to go on. She herself never considered giving up. She was paced at various times by her sister, Isak Helmy, the Egyptian, Lillian Cannon, and Louis Timson. The pounding of the seas wore out her pace-makers, but Miss Ederle kept on although sometimes forced to a slower stroke. Night was coming on when the lights of Dover began to flash through the rain. She herself said that she almost might have been asleep until she saw the lights and the bonfires which had been built on the shore....

It must have been a great moment in Gertrude Ederle's life when the water shallowed to the point where her feet found the sands of England beneath them. Wading ashore, she removed her bathing-cap and waved it at the crowd of about a thousand which had gathered on the beach to meet her. It was small wonder that she was happy for she had accomplished the ambition of her life and done what no woman had ever done before.

* * *

THE ANSWER TO A PRAYER

On April 12, 1955, amidst the popping of flash-bulbs and the grinding of television cameras, the public first learned that a young scientist named Jonas Salk had developed a vaccine to prevent paralytic poliomyelitis. In the University of Michigan's Rackham Building, Dr. Thomas Francis, Jr., read a report confirming the effectiveness of the vaccine. Outside, people observed moments of silence, rang bells, honked horns, blew factory whistles, fired salutes, closed schools and businesses and offered up their thanks in a thousand ways.

Ann Arbor, Mich., April 12 — The formal verdict on the Salk vaccine was disclosed today amid fanfare and drama far more typical of a Hollywood premiere than a medical meeting.

The event that made medical history took place in one of the University of Michigan's most glamorous structures — Rackham Building. Television cameras and radio microphones were set up outside the huge lecture hall. Inside the salmon-colored hall a battery of sixteen television and newsreel cameras were lined up across a long wooden platform especially built at the rear.

At 10:20 A.M. Dr. Thomas Francis Jr., director of the Poliomyelitis Vaccine Evaluation Center and the man of the hour, was introduced. A short, chunky man with a close-cropped mustache, he was wearing a black suit, white shirt and striped gray tie.

He stepped behind a lectern decorated with a blue and gold banner bearing the seal of the university. He appeared small, hidden up to his breast pocket by the lectern, as he looked out toward his audience of 500 scientists and physicians. Cameras ground and spotlights played upon him. Then Dr. Francis adjusted his horn-rimmed glasses and began to read his long-awaited report in a slow, conversational tone. It was the report of a meticulous and dedicated scientist, presented without dramatics.

Nevertheless, the moment was a dramatic one, no matter how hard the Professor of Epidemiology tried to make it otherwise with his charts and statistics and careful qualifications. The nation and the world had been waiting for this report, a report that could mean hope for millions of patients and a great step forward in the control of paralytic polio....

The audience was quiet and respectful. There were no bursts of applause. Even at the end of Dr. Francis' address, after he had made it clear that the Salk vaccine had been proved an effective weapon, the applause seemed restrained.

Outside the hall, however, the Hollywood atmosphere prevailed. Students and the curious crowded close behind television cameras set up for interviews with medical celebrities. In a press room three floors above, more than 150 newspaper, radio and television reporters were sending out details....

With Dr. Salk today in his hour of triumph were his wife, Mrs. Donna Salk, and three sons, Peter, 11 years old; Darrell, 8, and Jonathan, 5. The two older boys were among the first to be inoculated with the vaccine developed by their father.

Much attention was focused throughout the day on Dr. Salk, who had spent long hours in the laboratory to make this day possible.

Mrs. Salk seemed somewhat embarrassed by all the attention. She said that she and her family would be glad when things calmed down again and they could return to normal life.

* * *

Moments of Laughter,
Heartbreak and Inspiration

THERE'S A NEW STAR IN HEAVEN TONIGHT

The date was August 24, 1926, thereafter known as Mad Tuesday. It was the funeral day of Rudolph Valentino, of whom H. L. Mencken wrote, "Here was one who was catnip to women." A crowd numbering thirty thousand at its peak surged round the coffin at Campbell's Funeral Home. The way Irving Shulman tells it, the whole affair was a mixture of the tragic and bizarre.

Potted palms and luxurious ferns were arranged around the catafalque; a single red rose in a gilt bud vase supplied a touch of color behind Valentino's head. At a small altar, a statue of the Virgin was framed by scented candles, a tooled volume of the Vulgate Bible and a rosary. Because floral offerings had not yet arrived in quantity, appropriate bouquets and wreaths were moved in from Campbell's florist shop next door....

Newcomers continued to arrive, and many of them carried Thermos jugs, sandwiches and collapsible camp chairs. Newsboys and shoeshine boys appeared in strength and neighborhood urchins raided the local stores and markets for wooden boxes and crates, which they sold for quarters to those in the lines. As the crowd swelled and the supply of boxes diminished, the price rose to as much as three dollars. People from near-by apartment houses began to sell fruit and sand-wiches. A bustling trade in soft drinks, ice cream and lemon ices developed; platoons of frankfurter vendors exhausted their stock....

Soon after two o'clock, to the delight of the po-lice officers, it began to drizzle. Minutes later it was raining steadily and the more than fifteen thousand people now massed in the vicinity of Campbell's chanted in unison for the doors to be opened. Those fortunate enough to be near the doors of the chapel or its plate-glass windows be-gan to beat their fists against the bronze and glass as they demanded admission. Additional squads of police arrived, along with several police ser-geants and lieutenants, led by Captain Hammill, and pushed their way through and managed to enter while the officers already there beat back the crowd....

Psychologically blind, emotionally drunk, in-toxicated by steamy human contact, increasingly defiant of the impotent police force—the mob, transformed into a human juggernaut, stormed the doors. It shouted and screamed and cried out in a masochistic ecstasy that transmuted pain into joy. Step by step, three of the policemen gave ground until with a mighty surge the mob trapped them against the large plate-glass window. Then, as if it were a giant wave, it paused, gained a crest and broke against the policemen until the glass shattered, raining razor-sharp shards over the struggling policemen and the screaming mob.

Three policemen and two women fell through the broken window. Others lay stunned or unconscious, as the crowd continued to surge forward. To save the fallen, three mounted policemen charged desperately at the crowd until it fell back. Several men and women were trampled by the horses' hoofs as they attempted to duck under the animals' bellies.

At that moment the front doors of the Funeral Church opened and in the first mad rush the police officers detailed there were swept along with the milling crowd that knocked over potted palms, chairs and other furniture. Lamps fell and were trampled as the mob pushed toward the Gold Room, where Valentino lay. George Ullman, Valentino's manager, attempted to block them, as he shouted at the police to close the gates of the chapel. In the mounting confusion, yowling men and women clawed at each other, kicked and spat and struck out blindly, as they hurled themselves forward. They did not seem to hear or care that men and women were being dangerously trampled as they surged into the Gold Room and toward the catafalque, where for several terrible moments it appeared as if the draperies and casket might be spilled to the muddy carpet....

What confused the officers and inhibited their decisions were the circumstances of disorder. Most of this swarming mob was made up of people who had never before been and might never again be connected with any disturbance. They were not here to lynch, burn or protest but to pay last honors to a movie idol. They had come because the newspapers had said that Valentino wished his body to be viewed by his fans. Small radio stations in and around the city were also entreating their listeners to pay personal homage to the dead star, to dedicate one day of their lives as a tribute to the actor who had given them so many hours of love, affection and enjoyment.

★ ★ ★

END OF AN ERA

December 5, 1929. The night Prohibition died, America held an Irish wake. There were rowdy toasts, lots of laughter, two-bit drinks, and after all, there were some people sober in the morning.

New York, Dec. 5 — John Barleycorn came back to Broadway tonight from his 14-year exile. The town had changed, so had he.

He was not the bleary-eyed old man they drove into the wilderness fourteen years ago, but a restrained patriarch who realized apparently that his popularity depended on his decorum.

Dusk was here when he came tearing across the country from Utah, but even then the multitudes had gathered at Times Square to welcome him.

They watched the story unfold in the lights that tell the news on Broadway. There was no shouting, only the usual noises—the rumble of traffic, the clang and bustle of the street.

Ten thousand eyes were turned on Times Square's lights—

"Utah voting!" the sign flashed.

A lull: A policeman's horse pawed the pavement. The multitude shifted, swayed and sighed.

"Prohibition is dead!" the lights flickered.

The crowd whooped a few "hoorays," but it didn't roar. The letdown was obvious. It was all over but the shouting, but the throng didn't shout—it milled about and waited.

Newsboys took up the peal—"Prohibition is dead"—and a million lights repeated the story. Over on the Hudson, the frog-throated steamers began a sonorous symphony, a requiem for the era. The harbor boats whined prohibition's dirge, then began blasting salutes to John Barleycorn.

From the four corners, he came to town. Trucks began scurrying away from liquor wholesalers, careened through the streets and disgorged their liquors at hotels and restaurants and clubs.

Ships and planes brought it in—rum from Cuba, Scotch and rye from Canada, wines from France's slopes of gold, the Rhine, the vineyards of California....

Crowds were waiting at the licensed bars when the first drink was poured.

"A toast," said the barkeeper at the Hotel Astor,

which has license No. 1.

"To happiness and prosperity," echoed the revelers....

The Waldorf-Astoria's elaborate bar was crowded the first few minutes to watch the mixing of drinks which had to be consumed at tables. The Biltmore had 200 in the lobby waiting for bartenders to mix the first one....

The traffic became thick and tangled. Policemen made signals frantically. The crowds laughed and shuffled along, peeping in windows, pausing at bars.

The few retail stores that had received licenses had a big supply and did a rushing business. Aubrey Hollingsworth of Corona, L.I., claimed the distinction of being the first to buy a package of legal liquor. He made the purchase immediately after Utah voted....

The White Star liner Majestic, laden with 6,200 cases of spirits, hove into the harbor about an hour before prohibition died and authorities closed its bar off Ambrose lightship.

When the liner put in, some of the passengers, including Marc Connell, the playwright; Laura La Plante, actress, and Ethel Levy, comedienne, trooped down the gangplank with certain mysterious packages under their arms.

"What's in those packages?" asked the customs men.

"Liquor," they yelled.

"O.K." said the customs men....

The Art Students' League, holding a costume repeal ball, with reservations for more than 1,200, built its program around a hilarious funeral ceremony. At the stroke of midnight the coffin supposed to contain "Old Man Prohibition" was ordered opened, with a "beautiful female figure symbolic of the returning spirit of Bacchus stepping from it."

A Broadway dance hall started its celebration early in the afternoon by lynching "Old Man Prohibition" from the flagpole of its marquee. As several hundred persons watched, the effigy was jerked forty feet in the air.

A few minutes later it was lowered, placed in a white pine box and drawn down Broadway to Times Square by a camel. On the box was painted "Nobody's friend — everybody's fool on the way to Potter's Field F.O.B."

★ ★ ★

THE INVASION FROM MARS

Did you say bizarre? On Halloween night 1938, Orson Welles dramatized H.G. Wells's fantasy War of the Worlds, *in which Martian invaders descend to destroy our earth. Only trouble was, over a million panic-stricken people* believed *the broadcast. Here is their story.*

Long before the broadcast had ended, people all over the United States were praying, crying, fleeing frantically to escape death from the Martians. Some ran to rescue loved ones. Others telephoned farewells or warnings, hurried to inform neighbors, sought information from newspapers or radio stations, summoned ambulances and police cars....

"I knew it was something terrible and I was frightened," said Mrs. Ferguson, a northern New Jersey housewife, to the inquiring interviewer. "But I didn't know just what it was. I couldn't make myself believe it was the end of the world. I've always heard that when the world would come to an end, it would come so fast nobody would know—so why should God get in touch with this announcer?..."

Archie Burbank, a filling station operator in Newark, described his reactions. "My girl friend

Radio Listeners in Panic!

and I stayed in the car for awhile, just driving around. Then we followed the lead of a friend. All of us ran into a grocery store and asked the man if we could go into his cellar. He said, 'What's the matter? Are you trying to ruin my business?' So he chased us out. A crowd collected. We rushed to an apartment house and asked the man in the apartment to let us in his cellar. He said, 'I don't have any cellar! Get away!' Then people started to rush out of the apartment house all undressed. We got into the car and listened some more. Suddenly, the announcer was gassed, the station went dead so we tried another station but nothing would come on. Then we went to a gas station and filled up our tank in preparation for just riding as far as we could. The gas station man didn't know anything about it. Then one friend, male, decided he would call up the *Newark Evening News.* He found out it was a play. We listened to the rest of the play and then went dancing."...

Mrs. Delaney, an ardent Catholic living in a New York suburb, could not pull herself from her radio. "I never hugged my radio so closely as I did last night. I held a crucifix in my hand and prayed while looking out of my open window for falling meteors. I also wanted to get a faint whiff of the gas so that I would know when to close my window and hermetically seal my room with waterproof cement or anything else I could get hold of. My plan was to stay in the room and hope that I would not suffocate before the gas blew away....

Mothers all over the country hastened to protect helpless infants and children. From New England was sent the description of Mrs. Walters. "I kept shivering and shaking. I pulled out suitcases and put them back, started to pack, but didn't know what to take. I kept piling clothes on my baby, took all her clothes out and wrapped her up. Everybody went out of the house except the neighbors upstairs. I ran up and banged on his door. He wrapped two of his children in blankets and I carried the other, and my husband carried my child. We rushed out. I don't know why but I wanted to take some bread, for I thought that if everything is burning, you can't eat money, but you can eat bread."...

George Bates, an unskilled laborer in Massachusetts spent his savings trying to escape...."I thought the best thing to do was go away, so I took $3.25 out of my savings and bought a ticket. After I had gone 60 miles I heard it was a play. Now I don't have any money left for the shoes I was saving up for. Would you please have someone send me a pair of black shoes, size 9-B."

★ ★ ★

I HAVE A DREAM

The civil rights march to Washington in August, 1963, was one of the high points of Martin Luther King's life ambitions. He and his staff planned the strategy for the march with attention to even the smallest details. The speech which he delivered, portions of which follow, eloquently indicates why Martin Luther King was a legendary figure even before his tragic death.

I have a dream today.

I have a dream that one day every valley shall be exalted, every hill and mountain shall be made low, the rough places will be made plains, and the crooked places will be made straight, and the glory of the Lord shall be revealed, and all flesh shall see it together.

This is our hope. This is the faith with which I return to the South. With this faith we will be able to hew out of the mountain of despair a stone of hope. With this faith we will be able to transform the jangling discords of our nation into a beautiful symphony of brotherhood. With this faith we will be able to work together, to pray together, to struggle together, to go to jail together, to stand up for freedom together, knowing that we will be free one day.

This will be the day when all of God's children will be able to sing with new meaning "My country 'tis of thee, sweet land of liberty, of thee I sing. Land where my fathers died, land of the pilgrim's pride, from every mountainside, let freedom ring."

And if America is to be a great nation this must become true. So let freedom ring from the prodigious hilltops of New Hampshire. Let freedom ring from the mighty mountains of New York. Let freedom ring from the heightening Alleghenies of Pennsylvania!

Let freedom ring from the snowcapped Rockies of Colorado!

Let freedom ring from the curvacious peaks of California!

But not only that; let freedom ring from Stone Mountain of Georgia!

Let freedom ring from Lookout Mountain of Tennessee!

Let freedom ring from every hill and mole hill of Mississippi. From every mountainside, let freedom ring.

When we let freedom ring, when we let it ring from every village and every hamlet, from every state and every city, we will be able to speed up that day when all of God's children, black men and white men, Jews and Gentiles, Protestants and Catholics, will be able to join hands and sing in the words of the old Negro spiritual, "Free at last! free at last! thank God almighty, we are free at last!"

★ ★ ★

WHERE WILL IT END?

As author Paul Sann points out, the praise or blame for the invention of the miniskirt is decidedly hard to fix. In any event, 1964 is beloved of most red-blooded American men as "the year of the miniskirt."

...In the mid-Sixties...the flapper came all the way back, and the knee, sometimes worthy of a satisfying glance and sometimes in the proverbial housemaid's category, came back into view. The upward flight, slow and tentative, started in a couple of British and French fashion temples while such a formidable American stalwart as Pauline Trigere was stoutly refusing to snip any more off the hemlines of her models. But then the pace-setting Courrèges in Paris decided that there wasn't any reason why the girls shouldn't go all the way and let the knee show.

The miniskirt was upon us.

Is it all the fault of Courrèges?

The author put the question to Ruth Preston, fashion writer for the New York *Post,* and drew a pitying look, like he didn't know anything. "Courrèges, of course," Miss Preston said, but then she herself was assailed by doubts and it turned out that you could still get an argument over whether the French designer got there first — first with the *least,* that is — or whether it was all started by little Mary Quant in her Mod-Mod boutique, the Bazaar, in London's Chelsea District....

In any case, 1964 was indeed the year that the miniskirt got off the ground, so to speak, around the world....The chopped-off skirt, more like a bib worn below the waist, had its main appeal among the younger swingers, although an alert photographer from *Women's Wear Daily* caught nobody less than Jacqueline Kennedy emerging from a posh Manhattan restaurant in one of the new models on a crisp December day. Elizabeth Taylor also squeezed into the nonskirt, presumably with the full benediction of Richard Burton. And John V. Lindsay, the young-in-heart Mayor of New York, endorsed the bare knee even while his own fussy high school principals were bewailing it. "It's a functional thing," the Mayor said. "It enables young ladies to run faster, and because of it, they may have to."...Tallulah Bankhead, registering the same qualified endorsement, suggested that twenty-one would be a suitable age limit for the bare-knee set. "You'll never catch me wearing one, Dahling," the actress told columnist Leonard Lyons. "I have beautiful feet and ankles, but knees like Daddy's."...Without dwelling on the merits of that particular joint, Gina Lollobrigida set forth her own case against the miniskirt by saying that "it is better for men to discover than for women to reveal."

★ ★ ★

47

Elvis to be on Sullivan!

TRIBAL RHYTHMS!

He had four Cadillacs, a three-wheeled Messer-schmitt, two monkeys and a hit record. Who was he? He was Elvis Aron Presley, and his rock sound was the biggest change in music in decades. When he appeared on the Ed Sullivan show in 1956, the whole country tuned in and turned on to this swivel-hipped phenomenon.

A robust nineteen-year-old six-footer who looked more like Marlboro Country than metropolitan Tennessee, Elvis came off the truck and set out to climb the gold-plated Everest of Rock 'n' Roll. He arrived with a hip wriggle calculated to stir all kinds of instincts, motherly and beyond. That was in 1954, and within two years, on the strength of such record hits as "Blue Suede Shoes" and "Hound Dog," delivered in a driving rockabilly style reminiscent of the unsung Chuck Berry, the New York television impresarios came looking for him. Marshall McLuhan, something of a one-man fad himself in the Deepthink Sixties, has told us that the medium is the message and also that the medium is the massage. Elvis serves as an exhibit here, if one may risk a play on the Professor's sometimes cloudy words, for there was both message and massage in it when the hazel-eyed kid with the sideburns set the nation's television screens aflame....

Did NBC quail before the storm when its turn came? Of course not. The network, bless its corporate soul, observed that the reformed truck jockey had pushed Uncle Miltie's ratings past Phil Silvers' *Sergeant Bilko* for the first time and let Steve Allen book him in the all-important Sunday night spot against Ed Sullivan....He earned Allen 55.3 percent of the viewing audience against a staggeringly low 14.8 for its CBS rival. Sullivan, passed in the ratings for the first time since Dean Martin and Jerry Lewis had turned that trick two years before, read the Trendex on the wall and reached for his checkbook. Against the $5,500 Allen had paid to Presley, he went to Colonel Tom Parker, the old Tennessee carnival man who constitutes the Presley brain trust, and signed the singer for three appearances in the fall for a round $50,000. In the process, the outspoken columnist-maestro knew he would have to swallow some disdainful remarks he had made earlier about the hillbilly from Memphis. In character, Sullivan took back the bad words, said he would let the boy do his act without handcuffs, and steeled himself for the voices of protest. But while the anti-Presley legions were still in full cry, the people in the great wasteland obviously were waiting with bated breath for him to show up before the unblinking CBS camera. His first appearance with Sullivan, who did take the precaution of moving the cameras in above the waist when the boy lost his head and shook too much, skyrocketed the show to an eight-year high as an estimated 54,000,000 persons tuned in—a record due to stand until that Sunday in February, 1964, when the Beatles' American debut with Sullivan drew something like 67,500,000 viewers. Looking back, and bearing in mind that the advent of the Twist would bring all kinds of scantily clad Go-Go girls to the little screen…you have to wonder what all the fuss over Presley was about. In any event, there was no evidence anywhere, not even in the J. Edgar Hoover archives, that the merger of Elvis and Ed Sullivan had in itself prompted any noticeable outbreak of hubcap stealing, promiscuity or delinquency. Like nothing happened, man.

★   ★   ★

IWO JIMA

On February 19, 1945, the largest Marine force ever to go into battle began the assault on a tiny rock only seven hundred miles from Tokyo. Five weeks later the Stars and Stripes went up high atop Mt. Suribachi, Iwo Jima, last step to victory in the Pacific. Richard Newcomb details the drama of that moment.

Friday was the day to take Suribachi. The bald, gray dome, so formidable only a few days ago, was now still, the caves and chambers nearly empty, the blockhouses torn from their roots by the naval guns, the pillboxes blasted and agape, the tunnels closed and smoking.

Sergeant Sherman B. Watson of 2/28 set out at eight o'clock, scrambling up the north face with three privates from Company F: Louis Charlo, a Montana Indian, Theodore White of Kansas, and George Mercer from Iowa. Once out of the rubble at the base of the mountain, footing was good and they climbed up warily. It was very quiet, and in forty minutes they were at the cone, peering into the defunct crater. Nearby was a battery of heavy machine guns, ammunition stacked alongside it, but no Japanese. The patrol slid down the mountain to report.

Now was the time for Lieutenant Wells' flag. Colonel Johnson sent a runner for Lieutenant Harold G. Schrier, a slim, tall ex-Raider. When Schrier got to the battalion command post the colonel told him to seize the crest and hold it.

"And put this up on the hill," Johnson said, handing him the flag.

Schrier, executive officer of Company E, started out with 40 men, putting out flankers to cover the advance. The patrol was plainly visible as it moved up the face of the mountain, and all over the southern end of the island dirty, tired Marines watched.

"Those guys ought to be getting flight pay," said a bearded corporal.

Still there was no opposition, and at 10:15 Schrier and a small party of men tumbled over the rim into the crater. There were no Japanese in sight.

There, nearly 600 feet above the sea, a moment in history was taking shape.

The patrol scouted through the crater, rifles ready; a couple of the men found a piece of pipe, about 20 feet long. They lashed the flag to one end and thrust the other into soft ground near the north rim of the crater. The flag rose above the mountain, clearly visible from land and sea, and snapped out in a brisk wind. Sergeant Louis R. Lowery, a photographer for *Leatherneck* magazine, stood in the crater taking pictures....

As the shutter clicked, two Japanese darted from a cave. One threw a grenade and ran toward the flag, his sword drawn. [Private First Class James] Robeson shot him, and his body rolled down the inside of the crater, snapping off his sword under him. The other Japanese hurled a grenade toward Lowery, and the sergeant vaulted over the rim, sliding 50 feet down the mountain before he could stop. The camera was smashed, but the pictures were safe inside, and the flag was up. Six men raised it: Schrier, Platoon Sergeant Ernest I. Thomas, Jr.; Sergeant Henry O. Hansen, Corporal Charles W. Lindberg, Private First Class James R. Michels, and the Crow Indian, Private Charlo.

★ ★ ★

THE DAY
A PICTURE TALKED

Television has had an unprecedented impact on our culture. It is at once instructor and entertainer. It has been praised as "a cultural light" and vilified as a "wasteland." It is hard to believe that in 1927 no one knew what to do with it. Clearly it was a marvelous invention straight out of Jules Verne. The headline writer for the New York Times *was beside himself. "Far Off Speakers Seen As Well As Heard," he wrote. "Like a Photo Come to Life…First Time in History." April 7, 1927, marked the first public TV broadcast ever. The* Times *tells the story.*

Herbert Hoover made a speech in Washington yesterday afternoon. An audience in New York heard him and saw him.

More than 200 miles of space intervening between the speaker and his audience was annihilated by the television apparatus developed by the Bell Laboratories of the American Telephone and Telegraph Company and demonstrated publicly for the first time yesterday….

When the television pictures were thrown on a screen two by three inches, the likeness was excellent. It was as if a photograph had suddenly come to life and begun to talk, smile, nod its head

54

and look this way and that. When the screen was enlarged to two by three feet, the results were not so good....

The face looked up from the manuscript, the lips began to move and the first television-telephone speech started as follows:

"It is a matter of just pride to have a part in this historic occasion.

"We have long been familiar with the electrical transmission of sound. Today we have, in a sense, the transmission of sight, for the first time in the world's history.

"Human genius has now destroyed the impediment of distance in a new respect, and in a manner hitherto unknown. What its uses may finally be no one can tell, any more than man could foresee in past years the modern developments of the telegraph or the telephone. All we can say today is that there has been created a marvelous agency for whatever use the future may find, with the full realization that every great and fundamental discovery of the past has been followed by use far beyond the vision of its creator.

"Every school child is aware of the dramatic beginnings of the telegraph, the telephone and the radio, and this evolution in electrical communications has perhaps an importance as vital as any of these...."

Time as well as space was eliminated. Secretary Hoover's New York hearers and spectators were something like a thousandth part of a second later than the persons at his side in hearing him and in seeing changes of countenance....

In the second part of the program the group in New York saw and heard performances in the Whippany studio of the American Telephone and Telegraph Company by wireless. The first face flashed on the screen from Whippany, N.J., was that of E.L. Nelson, an engineer, who gave a technical description of what was taking place. Mr. Nelson had a good television face. He screened well as he talked.

Next came a vaudeville act by radio from Whippany. A. Dolan, a comedian, first appeared before the audience as a stage Irishman, with side whiskers and a broken pipe, and did a monologue in brogue. Then he made a quick change and came back in blackface with a new line of quips in Negro dialect. The loudspeaker part went over very well. It was the first vaudeville act that ever went on the air as a talking picture and in its possibilities it may be compared with the Fred Ott sneeze of more than thirty years ago, the first piece of comedy ever recorded in motion pictures. For the commercial future of television, if it has one, is thought to be largely in public entertainment — super-news reels flashed before audiences at the moment of occurrence, together with dramatic and musical acts shot on the ether waves in sound and picture at the instant they are taking place at the studio.

★   ★   ★

TWISTIN' U.S.A.

There were Chubby Checker T-shirts and jeans and ties, Chubby Checker dolls, Twist skirts and Twist raincoats and Twist nighties. It was a fad of rare proportion. According to devotee N. K. Cohn, it first gained national impetus in 1961 when the Peppermint Lounge in New York shuddered, shook, and gave birth to the most memorable of dances.

"I'm not easily shocked but the Twist shocked me ...half Negroid, half Manhattan, and when you see it on its native heath, wholly frightening. ...I can't believe that London will ever go to quite these extremes....the essence of the Twist, the curious perverted heart of it, is that you dance it alone": Beverley Nichols reporting from New York in January 1962....

...Most often it would have been a scraped grade-C fad, maximum span of six months. Another hula hoop. But 1961 was parched, was really desperate. So first Chubby Checker had a hit record. Second, New York smart society decided that the Twist was cute and started to hang out in the Peppermint Lounge. Third, the gossip columnists jumped aboard. Fourth, the whole industry started hyping. And fifth, madness set in....

The Twist wasn't even new. Hank Ballard, who had been around on the R&B scene ever since the early fifties, wrote the original song in 1958 and had a specialized hit with it. Dance-craze records have always been a stable part of the Negro market, and nobody paid much attention.

Two years on, Chubby Checker re-recorded it and got himself a national breakout. Checker was Ernest Evans from Philadelphia and had been a chicken-plucker. He looked something like a young Fats Domino, and he played it up; he even bowdlerized the fat man's name (Fats Domino = Chubby Checker: do you dig?). Truthfully, he wasn't much talented, but he was shrewd: he found himself with a hit on his hands and he hammered it. He twisted like a maniac. Demonstrated it on television, diagrammed it in the papers. Lost thirty-five pounds in a year just pretending to towel his back. So the Twist seemed almost fun, and it caught on. Journalists satirized it gently, how ludicrous and freak it was. The Peppermint Lounge, just off Times Square, hired a group called Joey Dee and the Starliters, and they played Twist all night every night. Chubby Checker cut *Let's Twist Again.* Even Elvis had a number one twist song, *Rock-A-Hula-Baby.* This was all getting to mean big business.

Here's where something odd happened. New York socialites, truly smart people, started to haunt the Peppermint Lounge. Elsa Maxwell and Greta Garbo and Judy Garland, Noel Coward and Tennessee Williams, the Duke of Bedford. Everyone, as they say, who was anyone. All of them twisting like there was no tomorrow and looking very foolish indeed. Inside weeks, you had to spray twenty-dollar bills like confetti even to catch a glimpse of the dance floor.

★ ★ ★

A LEGACY FOR TOMORROW

On February 21, 1972, Richard M. Nixon stood where no American president had stood before—on the soil of Communist China. His toast to the people of China was more than an act of diplomatic protocol; it was an eloquent plea for understanding between two great peoples of the world. It made history.

Mr. Prime Minister, I wish to thank you for your very gracious and eloquent remarks. At this very moment, through the wonders of telecommunications, more people are seeing and hearing what we say than on any other such occasion in the whole history of the world. Yet, what we say here will not be long remembered. What we do here can change the world.

As you said in your toast, the Chinese people are a great people, the American people are a great people. If our two people are enemies the future of this world we share together is dark indeed. But if we can find common ground to work together, the chance for world peace is immeasurably increased.

In the spirit of frankness which I hope will characterize our talks this week, let us recognize at the outset these points: We have at times in the past been enemies. We have great differences today. What brings us together is that we have common interests which transcend those differences. As we discuss our differences, neither of us will compromise our principles. But while we cannot close the gulf between us, we can try to bridge it so that we may be able to talk across it.

So, let us, in these next 5 days, start a long march together, not in lockstep, but on different roads leading to the same goal: the goal of building a world structure of peace and justice in which all may stand together with equal dignity and in which each nation, large or small, has a right to determine its own form of government, free of outside interference or domination. The world watches. The world listens. The world waits to see what we will do. What is the world? In a personal sense, I think of my eldest daughter, whose birthday is today. As I think of her, I think of all the children in the world, in Asia, in Africa, in Europe, in the Americas, most of whom were born since the date of the foundation of the People's Republic of China.

What legacy shall we leave our children? Are they destined to die for the hatreds which have plagued the old world, or are they destined to live because we had the vision to build a new world?

There is no reason for us to be enemies. Neither of us seeks the territory of the other; neither of us seeks domination over the other; neither of us seeks to stretch out our hands and rule the world.

Chairman Mao has written: "So many deeds cry out to be done, and always urgently. The world rolls on. Time passes. Ten thousand years are too long. Seize the day, seize the hour."

This is the hour. This is the day for our two peoples to rise to the heights of greatness which can build a new and a better world.

In that spirit, I ask all of you present to join me in raising your glasses to Chairman Mao, to Prime Minister Chou, and to the friendship of the Chinese and American people, which can lead to friendship and peace for all people in the world.

★   ★   ★

Set in Trump Medieval,
a Venetian typeface designed by
Professor Georg Trump, Munich.
Printed on Hallmark Eggshell Book paper.
Designed by Rainer K. Koenig.